W9-BKV-746

Máquinas maravillosas/Mighty Machines
Máquinas niveladoras/Bulldozers

por/by Linda D. Williams

Traducción/Translation: Martín Luis Guzmán Ferrer, Ph.D.
Editor Consultor/Consulting Editor: Dra. Gail Saunders-Smith

Consultant: Debra Hilmerson, Member
American Society of Safety Engineers
Des Plaines, Illinois

Capstone
press

Mankato, Minnesota

Pebble Plus is published by Capstone Press
151 Good Counsel Drive, P.O. Box 669, Mankato, Minnesota 56002
www.capstonepress.com

1 2 3 4 5 6 11 10 09 08 07 06

Library of Congress Cataloging-in-Publication Data
Williams, Linda D.
   [Bulldozers. Spanish and English]
   Máquinas niveladoras=Bulldozers/by Linda D. Williams.
   p. cm.—(Pebble plus. Máquinas maravillosas=Pebble plus. Mighty machines)
   Includes index.
   ISBN-13: 978-0-7368-5867-0 (hardcover)
   ISBN-10: 0-7368-5867-9 (hardcover)
   Bulldozers—Juvenile literature. I. Title. II. Series: Pebble Plus. Máquinas maravillosas.
TA725.W3518 2006
629.225—dc22   2005019049

Summary: Simple text and photographs present bulldozers and the work they do.

Editorial Credits
Martha E. H. Rustad, editor; Jenny Marks, bilingual editor; Eida del Risco, Spanish copy editor; Molly Nei,
   series designer; Scott Thoms, photo researcher; Karen Hieb, product planning editor

Photo Credits
Bruce Coleman Inc./Keith Gunnar, 13
Capstone Press Archive, 6–7, 10–11
constructionphotography.com, 14–15, 21
Corbis/Lester Lefkowitz, cover; Lowell Georgia, 16–17; Royalty Free, 18–19
DAVID R. FRAZIER Photolibrary, 1, 8–9
Folio, Inc./Ira Wexler, 5

Note to Parents and Teachers

The Mighty Machines series supports national standards related to science, technology, and society. This book describes and illustrates bulldozers. The images support early readers in understanding the text. The repetition of words and phrases helps early readers learn new words. This book also introduces early readers to subject-specific vocabulary words, which are defined in the Glossary section. Early readers may need assistance to read some words and to use the Table of Contents, Glossary, Internet Sites, and Index sections of the book.

Table of Contents

Tabla de contenidos

Bulldozers

Bulldozers push. Bulldozers
change the shape of
the land.

Máquinas niveladoras

Las niveladoras sirven para
empujar. Las niveladoras
cambian la forma del terreno.

Parts of Bulldozers

Bulldozers have wide
blades. Blades push dirt
into piles.

Las partes de las máquinas niveladoras

Las niveladoras tienen unas palas
anchas. Con la tierra que empujan,
las niveladoras hacen montones.

6

blade/pala

Bulldozer drivers sit high up
in cabs. Drivers use
levers to lift and lower
the blades.

Los conductores de las niveladoras
se sientan en cabinas que están en
la parte de arriba de la niveladora.
Los conductores utilizan las palancas
para levantar y bajar los palas.

cab/cabina

Bulldozers move on tracks.
Tracks keep bulldozers
from getting stuck.

Las niveladoras se mueven
sobre bandas. Las bandas
impiden que la niveladora
se atasque.

track/banda

What Bulldozers Do

Bulldozers shove and
smooth. They push trees
and rocks out of the way.

Qué hacen las máquinas niveladoras

Las niveladoras rebajan
y aplanan el terreno. Empujan
los árboles y las piedras
que encuentran en su camino.

Bulldozers flatten bumps.
They make the ground flat
for roads.

Las niveladoras aplanan
los desniveles del terreno.
Dejan la tierra plana
para las carreteras.

Bulldozers push snow.
They clear roads
for cars and trucks.

Las niveladoras empujan
la nieve. Dejan las carreteras
limpias para los autos
y los camiones.

Bulldozers push garbage
in landfills. They cover
garbage with dirt.

Las niveladoras empujan
la basura en los vertederos.
Cubren la basura con tierra.

Mighty Machines

Bulldozers push
dirt. Bulldozers are
mighty machines.

Máquinas
maravillosas

Las niveladoras empujan la
tierra. Las niveladoras son
unas máquinas maravillosas.

Glossary

blade—a wide, curved piece of metal on a bulldozer; the blade pushes, scrapes, or lifts rocks and dirt.

cab—an area for a driver to sit in a large truck or machine, such as a bulldozer

garbage—most of the items that people throw away; other words for garbage are trash and waste.

landfill—a place where garbage is dumped and then buried; the garbage is buried between layers of dirt to protect the earth and water supply.

lever—a bar or handle used to control a machine

track—a wide metal belt that runs around wheels; a bulldozer uses two tracks to move over rough ground.

Glosario

banda—cinturón ancho de metal que se mueve sobre ruedas; la niveladora emplea dos bandas para moverse sobre terrenos irregulares.

basura—la mayoría de los artículos que las personas tiran; otras palabras para basura son sobras y desperdicios.

cabina—lugar donde se sienta el conductor en un camión o máquina, como una niveladora

pala—pieza de metal ancha y curva de la niveladora; la pala empuja, recoge o levanta piedras y tierra.

palanca—barra o manija que se emplea para controlar una máquina

vertedero—lugar donde se pone y se entierra la basura; la basura se entierra entre capas de tierra para proteger el suelo y las reservas de agua.

Internet Sites

FactHound offers a safe, fun way to find Internet sites related to this book. All of the sites on FactHound have been researched by our staff.

Here's how:

1) Visit *www.facthound.com*

2) Type in this special code **0736825932** for age-appropriate sites. Or enter a search word related to this book for a more general search.

3) Click on the **FETCH IT** button.

FactHound will fetch the best sites for you!

Sitios de Internet

FactHound te ofrece una manera segura y divertida para encontrar sitios de Internet relacionados con este libro. Todos los sitios de FactHound han sido investigados por nuestro equipo. Es posible que los sitios no estén en español.

Así:

1) Ve a *www.facthound.com*

2) Teclea la clave especial **0736825932** para los sitios apropiados por edad. O teclea una palabra relacionada con este libro para una búsqueda más general.

3) Clic en el botón de **FETCH IT**.

¡FactHound buscará los mejores sitios para ti!

Index

Índice